This notebook belongs to:

Tag us @authorsignite · AuthorsIgnite.com

www.authorsignite.com

If you find this notebook helpful,
we'd appreciate a positive review.

Please visit *authorsignite.com/products*
for gifts for yourself and others.

Thank you for supporting our small business!

Debra Brown, Meredith Brown, and Jessica Nash

Engage · Elevate · Empower

DESIGNED AND MADE IN THE USA

ISBN: 978-1-7341456-4-9

igniumpress

PAGE	TABLE OF CONTENTS

PAGE	TABLE OF CONTENTS

PAGE	TABLE OF CONTENTS

PAGE	TABLE OF CONTENTS

ideas & inspirations

SKETCHES, NOTES, IDEAS, INSPIRATION, THOUGHTS,
LISTS, DREAMS, HOPES, GOALS, PLANS, POSSIBILITIES...

JAN FEB MAR APR MAY JUN JUL AUG SEP OCT NOV DEC

1 2 3 4 5 6 7 8 9 10 11 12 13 14 15 16 17 18 19 20 21 22 23 24 25 26 27 28 29 30 31

JAN FEB MAR APR MAY JUN JUL AUG SEP OCT NOV DEC

1 2 3 4 5 6 7 8 9 10 11 12 13 14 15 16 17 18 19 20 21 22 23 24 25 26 27 28 29 30 31

JAN FEB MAR APR MAY JUN JUL AUG SEP OCT NOV DEC

1 2 3 4 5 6 7 8 9 10 11 12 13 14 15 16 17 18 19 20 21 22 23 24 25 26 27 28 29 30 31

JAN FEB MAR APR MAY JUN JUL AUG SEP OCT NOV DEC

1 2 3 4 5 6 7 8 9 10 11 12 13 14 15 16 17 18 19 20 21 22 23 24 25 26 27 28 29 30 31

JAN FEB MAR APR MAY JUN JUL AUG SEP OCT NOV DEC

1 2 3 4 5 6 7 8 9 10 11 12 13 14 15 16 17 18 19 20 21 22 23 24 25 26 27 28 29 30 31

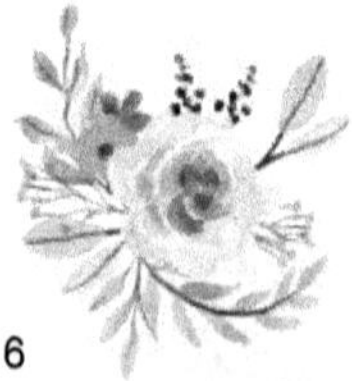

JAN FEB MAR APR MAY JUN JUL AUG SEP OCT NOV DEC

1 2 3 4 5 6 7 8 9 10 11 12 13 14 15 16 17 18 19 20 21 22 23 24 25 26 27 28 29 30 31

JAN FEB MAR APR MAY JUN JUL AUG SEP OCT NOV DEC

1 2 3 4 5 6 7 8 9 10 11 12 13 14 15 16 17 18 19 20 21 22 23 24 25 26 27 28 29 30 31

JAN FEB MAR APR MAY JUN JUL AUG SEP OCT NOV DEC

1 2 3 4 5 6 7 8 9 10 11 12 13 14 15 16 17 18 19 20 21 22 23 24 25 26 27 28 29 30 31

JAN FEB MAR APR MAY JUN JUL AUG SEP OCT NOV DEC

1 2 3 4 5 6 7 8 9 10 11 12 13 14 15 16 17 18 19 20 21 22 23 24 25 26 27 28 29 30 31

JAN FEB MAR APR MAY JUN JUL AUG SEP OCT NOV DEC

1 2 3 4 5 6 7 8 9 10 11 12 13 14 15 16 17 18 19 20 21 22 23 24 25 26 27 28 29 30 31

JAN FEB MAR APR MAY JUN JUL AUG SEP OCT NOV DEC

1 2 3 4 5 6 7 8 9 10 11 12 13 14 15 16 17 18 19 20 21 22 23 24 25 26 27 28 29 30 31

JAN FEB MAR APR MAY JUN JUL AUG SEP OCT NOV DEC

1 2 3 4 5 6 7 8 9 10 11 12 13 14 15 16 17 18 19 20 21 22 23 24 25 26 27 28 29 30 31

JAN FEB MAR APR MAY JUN JUL AUG SEP OCT NOV DEC

1 2 3 4 5 6 7 8 9 10 11 12 13 14 15 16 17 18 19 20 21 22 23 24 25 26 27 28 29 30 31

JAN FEB MAR APR MAY JUN JUL AUG SEP OCT NOV DEC

1 2 3 4 5 6 7 8 9 10 11 12 13 14 15 16 17 18 19 20 21 22 23 24 25 26 27 28 29 30 31

JAN FEB MAR APR MAY JUN JUL AUG SEP OCT NOV DEC

1 2 3 4 5 6 7 8 9 10 11 12 13 14 15 16 17 18 19 20 21 22 23 24 25 26 27 28 29 30 31

JAN FEB MAR APR MAY JUN JUL AUG SEP OCT NOV DEC

1 2 3 4 5 6 7 8 9 10 11 12 13 14 15 16 17 18 19 20 21 22 23 24 25 26 27 28 29 30 31

JAN FEB MAR APR MAY JUN JUL AUG SEP OCT NOV DEC

1 2 3 4 5 6 7 8 9 10 11 12 13 14 15 16 17 18 19 20 21 22 23 24 25 26 27 28 29 30 31

JAN FEB MAR APR MAY JUN JUL AUG SEP OCT NOV DEC

1 2 3 4 5 6 7 8 9 10 11 12 13 14 15 16 17 18 19 20 21 22 23 24 25 26 27 28 29 30 31

JAN FEB MAR APR MAY JUN JUL AUG SEP OCT NOV DEC

1 2 3 4 5 6 7 8 9 10 11 12 13 14 15 16 17 18 19 20 21 22 23 24 25 26 27 28 29 30 31

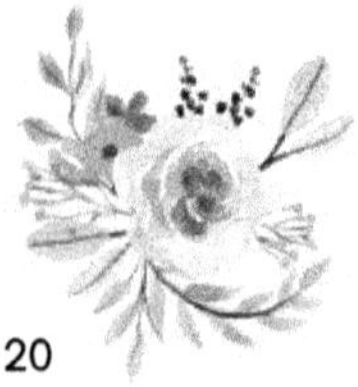

JAN FEB MAR APR MAY JUN JUL AUG SEP OCT NOV DEC

1 2 3 4 5 6 7 8 9 10 11 12 13 14 15 16 17 18 19 20 21 22 23 24 25 26 27 28 29 30 31

JAN FEB MAR APR MAY JUN JUL AUG SEP OCT NOV DEC

1 2 3 4 5 6 7 8 9 10 11 12 13 14 15 16 17 18 19 20 21 22 23 24 25 26 27 28 29 30 31

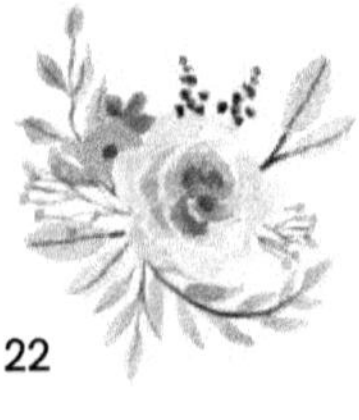

JAN FEB MAR APR MAY JUN JUL AUG SEP OCT NOV DEC

1 2 3 4 5 6 7 8 9 10 11 12 13 14 15 16 17 18 19 20 21 22 23 24 25 26 27 28 29 30 31

JAN FEB MAR APR MAY JUN JUL AUG SEP OCT NOV DEC

1 2 3 4 5 6 7 8 9 10 11 12 13 14 15 16 17 18 19 20 21 22 23 24 25 26 27 28 29 30 31

JAN FEB MAR APR MAY JUN JUL AUG SEP OCT NOV DEC

1 2 3 4 5 6 7 8 9 10 11 12 13 14 15 16 17 18 19 20 21 22 23 24 25 26 27 28 29 30 31

JAN FEB MAR APR MAY JUN JUL AUG SEP OCT NOV DEC

1 2 3 4 5 6 7 8 9 10 11 12 13 14 15 16 17 18 19 20 21 22 23 24 25 26 27 28 29 30 31

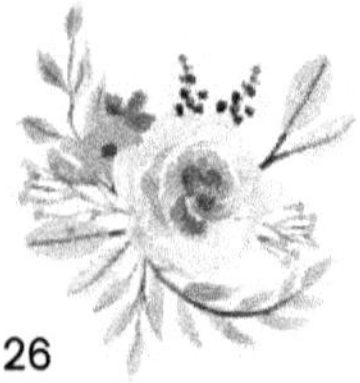

JAN FEB MAR APR MAY JUN JUL AUG SEP OCT NOV DEC

1 2 3 4 5 6 7 8 9 10 11 12 13 14 15 16 17 18 19 20 21 22 23 24 25 26 27 28 29 30 31

JAN FEB MAR APR MAY JUN JUL AUG SEP OCT NOV DEC

1 2 3 4 5 6 7 8 9 10 11 12 13 14 15 16 17 18 19 20 21 22 23 24 25 26 27 28 29 30 31

JAN FEB MAR APR MAY JUN JUL AUG SEP OCT NOV DEC

1 2 3 4 5 6 7 8 9 10 11 12 13 14 15 16 17 18 19 20 21 22 23 24 25 26 27 28 29 30 31

JAN FEB MAR APR MAY JUN JUL AUG SEP OCT NOV DEC

1 2 3 4 5 6 7 8 9 10 11 12 13 14 15 16 17 18 19 20 21 22 23 24 25 26 27 28 29 30 31

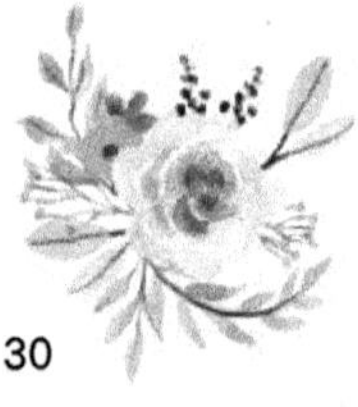

JAN FEB MAR APR MAY JUN JUL AUG SEP OCT NOV DEC

1 2 3 4 5 6 7 8 9 10 11 12 13 14 15 16 17 18 19 20 21 22 23 24 25 26 27 28 29 30 31

JAN FEB MAR APR MAY JUN JUL AUG SEP OCT NOV DEC

1 2 3 4 5 6 7 8 9 10 11 12 13 14 15 16 17 18 19 20 21 22 23 24 25 26 27 28 29 30 31

JAN FEB MAR APR MAY JUN JUL AUG SEP OCT NOV DEC

1 2 3 4 5 6 7 8 9 10 11 12 13 14 15 16 17 18 19 20 21 22 23 24 25 26 27 28 29 30 31

JAN FEB MAR APR MAY JUN JUL AUG SEP OCT NOV DEC

1 2 3 4 5 6 7 8 9 10 11 12 13 14 15 16 17 18 19 20 21 22 23 24 25 26 27 28 29 30 31

JAN FEB MAR APR MAY JUN JUL AUG SEP OCT NOV DEC

1 2 3 4 5 6 7 8 9 10 11 12 13 14 15 16 17 18 19 20 21 22 23 24 25 26 27 28 29 30 31

JAN FEB MAR APR MAY JUN JUL AUG SEP OCT NOV DEC

1 2 3 4 5 6 7 8 9 10 11 12 13 14 15 16 17 18 19 20 21 22 23 24 25 26 27 28 29 30 31

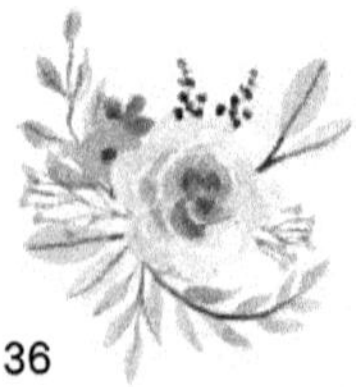

JAN FEB MAR APR MAY JUN JUL AUG SEP OCT NOV DEC

1 2 3 4 5 6 7 8 9 10 11 12 13 14 15 16 17 18 19 20 21 22 23 24 25 26 27 28 29 30 31

JAN FEB MAR APR MAY JUN JUL AUG SEP OCT NOV DEC

1 2 3 4 5 6 7 8 9 10 11 12 13 14 15 16 17 18 19 20 21 22 23 24 25 26 27 28 29 30 31

JAN FEB MAR APR MAY JUN JUL AUG SEP OCT NOV DEC

1 2 3 4 5 6 7 8 9 10 11 12 13 14 15 16 17 18 19 20 21 22 23 24 25 26 27 28 29 30 31

JAN FEB MAR APR MAY JUN JUL AUG SEP OCT NOV DEC

1 2 3 4 5 6 7 8 9 10 11 12 13 14 15 16 17 18 19 20 21 22 23 24 25 26 27 28 29 30 31

JAN FEB MAR APR MAY JUN JUL AUG SEP OCT NOV DEC

1 2 3 4 5 6 7 8 9 10 11 12 13 14 15 16 17 18 19 20 21 22 23 24 25 26 27 28 29 30 31

JAN FEB MAR APR MAY JUN JUL AUG SEP OCT NOV DEC

1 2 3 4 5 6 7 8 9 10 11 12 13 14 15 16 17 18 19 20 21 22 23 24 25 26 27 28 29 30 31

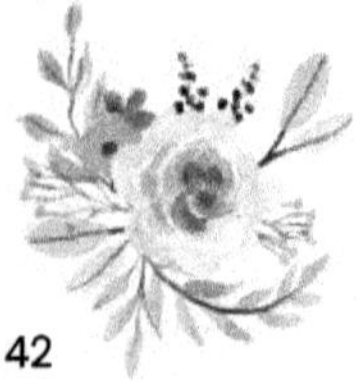

JAN FEB MAR APR MAY JUN JUL AUG SEP OCT NOV DEC

1 2 3 4 5 6 7 8 9 10 11 12 13 14 15 16 17 18 19 20 21 22 23 24 25 26 27 28 29 30 31

JAN FEB MAR APR MAY JUN JUL AUG SEP OCT NOV DEC

1 2 3 4 5 6 7 8 9 10 11 12 13 14 15 16 17 18 19 20 21 22 23 24 25 26 27 28 29 30 31

JAN FEB MAR APR MAY JUN JUL AUG SEP OCT NOV DEC

1 2 3 4 5 6 7 8 9 10 11 12 13 14 15 16 17 18 19 20 21 22 23 24 25 26 27 28 29 30 31

JAN FEB MAR APR MAY JUN JUL AUG SEP OCT NOV DEC

1 2 3 4 5 6 7 8 9 10 11 12 13 14 15 16 17 18 19 20 21 22 23 24 25 26 27 28 29 30 31

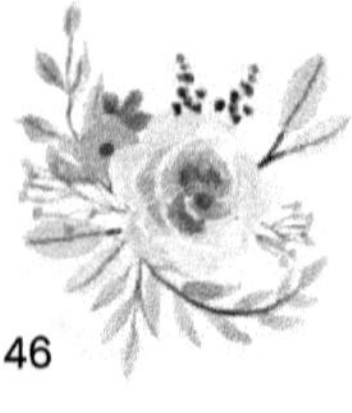

JAN FEB MAR APR MAY JUN JUL AUG SEP OCT NOV DEC

1 2 3 4 5 6 7 8 9 10 11 12 13 14 15 16 17 18 19 20 21 22 23 24 25 26 27 28 29 30 31

JAN FEB MAR APR MAY JUN JUL AUG SEP OCT NOV DEC

1 2 3 4 5 6 7 8 9 10 11 12 13 14 15 16 17 18 19 20 21 22 23 24 25 26 27 28 29 30 31

JAN FEB MAR APR MAY JUN JUL AUG SEP OCT NOV DEC

1 2 3 4 5 6 7 8 9 10 11 12 13 14 15 16 17 18 19 20 21 22 23 24 25 26 27 28 29 30 31

JAN FEB MAR APR MAY JUN JUL AUG SEP OCT NOV DEC

1 2 3 4 5 6 7 8 9 10 11 12 13 14 15 16 17 18 19 20 21 22 23 24 25 26 27 28 29 30 31

JAN FEB MAR APR MAY JUN JUL AUG SEP OCT NOV DEC

1 2 3 4 5 6 7 8 9 10 11 12 13 14 15 16 17 18 19 20 21 22 23 24 25 26 27 28 29 30 31

JAN FEB MAR APR MAY JUN JUL AUG SEP OCT NOV DEC

1 2 3 4 5 6 7 8 9 10 11 12 13 14 15 16 17 18 19 20 21 22 23 24 25 26 27 28 29 30 31

JAN FEB MAR APR MAY JUN JUL AUG SEP OCT NOV DEC

1 2 3 4 5 6 7 8 9 10 11 12 13 14 15 16 17 18 19 20 21 22 23 24 25 26 27 28 29 30 31

JAN FEB MAR APR MAY JUN JUL AUG SEP OCT NOV DEC

1 2 3 4 5 6 7 8 9 10 11 12 13 14 15 16 17 18 19 20 21 22 23 24 25 26 27 28 29 30 31

JAN FEB MAR APR MAY JUN JUL AUG SEP OCT NOV DEC

1 2 3 4 5 6 7 8 9 10 11 12 13 14 15 16 17 18 19 20 21 22 23 24 25 26 27 28 29 30 31

JAN FEB MAR APR MAY JUN JUL AUG SEP OCT NOV DEC
1 2 3 4 5 6 7 8 9 10 11 12 13 14 15 16 17 18 19 20 21 22 23 24 25 26 27 28 29 30 31

JAN FEB MAR APR MAY JUN JUL AUG SEP OCT NOV DEC

1 2 3 4 5 6 7 8 9 10 11 12 13 14 15 16 17 18 19 20 21 22 23 24 25 26 27 28 29 30 31

JAN FEB MAR APR MAY JUN JUL AUG SEP OCT NOV DEC

1 2 3 4 5 6 7 8 9 10 11 12 13 14 15 16 17 18 19 20 21 22 23 24 25 26 27 28 29 30 31

JAN FEB MAR APR MAY JUN JUL AUG SEP OCT NOV DEC

1 2 3 4 5 6 7 8 9 10 11 12 13 14 15 16 17 18 19 20 21 22 23 24 25 26 27 28 29 30 31

JAN FEB MAR APR MAY JUN JUL AUG SEP OCT NOV DEC

1 2 3 4 5 6 7 8 9 10 11 12 13 14 15 16 17 18 19 20 21 22 23 24 25 26 27 28 29 30 31

JAN FEB MAR APR MAY JUN JUL AUG SEP OCT NOV DEC

1 2 3 4 5 6 7 8 9 10 11 12 13 14 15 16 17 18 19 20 21 22 23 24 25 26 27 28 29 30 31

JAN FEB MAR APR MAY JUN JUL AUG SEP OCT NOV DEC

1 2 3 4 5 6 7 8 9 10 11 12 13 14 15 16 17 18 19 20 21 22 23 24 25 26 27 28 29 30 31

JAN FEB MAR APR MAY JUN JUL AUG SEP OCT NOV DEC

1 2 3 4 5 6 7 8 9 10 11 12 13 14 15 16 17 18 19 20 21 22 23 24 25 26 27 28 29 30 31

JAN FEB MAR APR MAY JUN JUL AUG SEP OCT NOV DEC

1 2 3 4 5 6 7 8 9 10 11 12 13 14 15 16 17 18 19 20 21 22 23 24 25 26 27 28 29 30 31

JAN FEB MAR APR MAY JUN JUL AUG SEP OCT NOV DEC

1 2 3 4 5 6 7 8 9 10 11 12 13 14 15 16 17 18 19 20 21 22 23 24 25 26 27 28 29 30 31

JAN FEB MAR APR MAY JUN JUL AUG SEP OCT NOV DEC

1 2 3 4 5 6 7 8 9 10 11 12 13 14 15 16 17 18 19 20 21 22 23 24 25 26 27 28 29 30 31

JAN FEB MAR APR MAY JUN JUL AUG SEP OCT NOV DEC

1 2 3 4 5 6 7 8 9 10 11 12 13 14 15 16 17 18 19 20 21 22 23 24 25 26 27 28 29 30 31

JAN FEB MAR APR MAY JUN JUL AUG SEP OCT NOV DEC

1 2 3 4 5 6 7 8 9 10 11 12 13 14 15 16 17 18 19 20 21 22 23 24 25 26 27 28 29 30 31

JAN FEB MAR APR MAY JUN JUL AUG SEP OCT NOV DEC

1 2 3 4 5 6 7 8 9 10 11 12 13 14 15 16 17 18 19 20 21 22 23 24 25 26 27 28 29 30 31

JAN FEB MAR APR MAY JUN JUL AUG SEP OCT NOV DEC

1 2 3 4 5 6 7 8 9 10 11 12 13 14 15 16 17 18 19 20 21 22 23 24 25 26 27 28 29 30 31

JAN FEB MAR APR MAY JUN JUL AUG SEP OCT NOV DEC

1 2 3 4 5 6 7 8 9 10 11 12 13 14 15 16 17 18 19 20 21 22 23 24 25 26 27 28 29 30 31

JAN FEB MAR APR MAY JUN JUL AUG SEP OCT NOV DEC

1 2 3 4 5 6 7 8 9 10 11 12 13 14 15 16 17 18 19 20 21 22 23 24 25 26 27 28 29 30 31

JAN FEB MAR APR MAY JUN JUL AUG SEP OCT NOV DEC

1 2 3 4 5 6 7 8 9 10 11 12 13 14 15 16 17 18 19 20 21 22 23 24 25 26 27 28 29 30 31

JAN FEB MAR APR MAY JUN JUL AUG SEP OCT NOV DEC

1 2 3 4 5 6 7 8 9 10 11 12 13 14 15 16 17 18 19 20 21 22 23 24 25 26 27 28 29 30 31

JAN FEB MAR APR MAY JUN JUL AUG SEP OCT NOV DEC

1 2 3 4 5 6 7 8 9 10 11 12 13 14 15 16 17 18 19 20 21 22 23 24 25 26 27 28 29 30 31

JAN FEB MAR APR MAY JUN JUL AUG SEP OCT NOV DEC

1 2 3 4 5 6 7 8 9 10 11 12 13 14 15 16 17 18 19 20 21 22 23 24 25 26 27 28 29 30 31

JAN FEB MAR APR MAY JUN JUL AUG SEP OCT NOV DEC

1 2 3 4 5 6 7 8 9 10 11 12 13 14 15 16 17 18 19 20 21 22 23 24 25 26 27 28 29 30 31

JAN FEB MAR APR MAY JUN JUL AUG SEP OCT NOV DEC

1 2 3 4 5 6 7 8 9 10 11 12 13 14 15 16 17 18 19 20 21 22 23 24 25 26 27 28 29 30 31

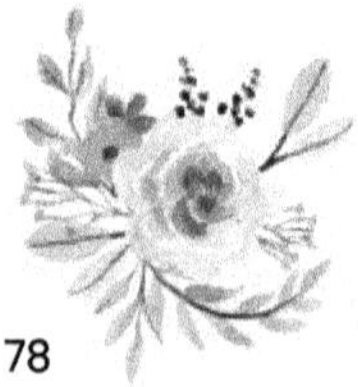

JAN FEB MAR APR MAY JUN JUL AUG SEP OCT NOV DEC

1 2 3 4 5 6 7 8 9 10 11 12 13 14 15 16 17 18 19 20 21 22 23 24 25 26 27 28 29 30 31

JAN FEB MAR APR MAY JUN JUL AUG SEP OCT NOV DEC

1 2 3 4 5 6 7 8 9 10 11 12 13 14 15 16 17 18 19 20 21 22 23 24 25 26 27 28 29 30 31

JAN FEB MAR APR MAY JUN JUL AUG SEP OCT NOV DEC

1 2 3 4 5 6 7 8 9 10 11 12 13 14 15 16 17 18 19 20 21 22 23 24 25 26 27 28 29 30 31

JAN FEB MAR APR MAY JUN JUL AUG SEP OCT NOV DEC

1 2 3 4 5 6 7 8 9 10 11 12 13 14 15 16 17 18 19 20 21 22 23 24 25 26 27 28 29 30 31

JAN FEB MAR APR MAY JUN JUL AUG SEP OCT NOV DEC

1 2 3 4 5 6 7 8 9 10 11 12 13 14 15 16 17 18 19 20 21 22 23 24 25 26 27 28 29 30 31

JAN FEB MAR APR MAY JUN JUL AUG SEP OCT NOV DEC

1 2 3 4 5 6 7 8 9 10 11 12 13 14 15 16 17 18 19 20 21 22 23 24 25 26 27 28 29 30 31

JAN FEB MAR APR MAY JUN JUL AUG SEP OCT NOV DEC

1 2 3 4 5 6 7 8 9 10 11 12 13 14 15 16 17 18 19 20 21 22 23 24 25 26 27 28 29 30 31

JAN FEB MAR APR MAY JUN JUL AUG SEP OCT NOV DEC

1 2 3 4 5 6 7 8 9 10 11 12 13 14 15 16 17 18 19 20 21 22 23 24 25 26 27 28 29 30 31

JAN FEB MAR APR MAY JUN JUL AUG SEP OCT NOV DEC

1 2 3 4 5 6 7 8 9 10 11 12 13 14 15 16 17 18 19 20 21 22 23 24 25 26 27 28 29 30 31

JAN FEB MAR APR MAY JUN JUL AUG SEP OCT NOV DEC

1 2 3 4 5 6 7 8 9 10 11 12 13 14 15 16 17 18 19 20 21 22 23 24 25 26 27 28 29 30 31

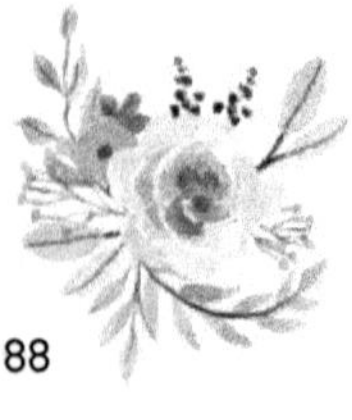

JAN FEB MAR APR MAY JUN JUL AUG SEP OCT NOV DEC

1 2 3 4 5 6 7 8 9 10 11 12 13 14 15 16 17 18 19 20 21 22 23 24 25 26 27 28 29 30 31

JAN FEB MAR APR MAY JUN JUL AUG SEP OCT NOV DEC

1 2 3 4 5 6 7 8 9 10 11 12 13 14 15 16 17 18 19 20 21 22 23 24 25 26 27 28 29 30 31

JAN FEB MAR APR MAY JUN JUL AUG SEP OCT NOV DEC

1 2 3 4 5 6 7 8 9 10 11 12 13 14 15 16 17 18 19 20 21 22 23 24 25 26 27 28 29 30 31

JAN FEB MAR APR MAY JUN JUL AUG SEP OCT NOV DEC

1 2 3 4 5 6 7 8 9 10 11 12 13 14 15 16 17 18 19 20 21 22 23 24 25 26 27 28 29 30 31

JAN FEB MAR APR MAY JUN JUL AUG SEP OCT NOV DEC

1 2 3 4 5 6 7 8 9 10 11 12 13 14 15 16 17 18 19 20 21 22 23 24 25 26 27 28 29 30 31

JAN FEB MAR APR MAY JUN JUL AUG SEP OCT NOV DEC

1 2 3 4 5 6 7 8 9 10 11 12 13 14 15 16 17 18 19 20 21 22 23 24 25 26 27 28 29 30 31

JAN FEB MAR APR MAY JUN JUL AUG SEP OCT NOV DEC

1 2 3 4 5 6 7 8 9 10 11 12 13 14 15 16 17 18 19 20 21 22 23 24 25 26 27 28 29 30 31

JAN FEB MAR APR MAY JUN JUL AUG SEP OCT NOV DEC
1 2 3 4 5 6 7 8 9 10 11 12 13 14 15 16 17 18 19 20 21 22 23 24 25 26 27 28 29 30 31

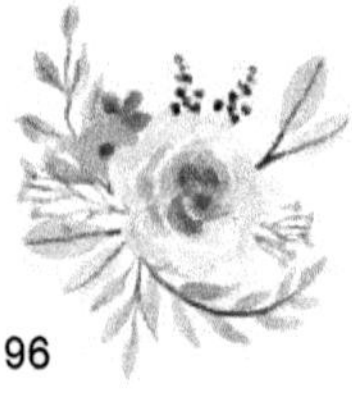

JAN FEB MAR APR MAY JUN JUL AUG SEP OCT NOV DEC

1 2 3 4 5 6 7 8 9 10 11 12 13 14 15 16 17 18 19 20 21 22 23 24 25 26 27 28 29 30 31

JAN FEB MAR APR MAY JUN JUL AUG SEP OCT NOV DEC

1 2 3 4 5 6 7 8 9 10 11 12 13 14 15 16 17 18 19 20 21 22 23 24 25 26 27 28 29 30 31

JAN FEB MAR APR MAY JUN JUL AUG SEP OCT NOV DEC

1 2 3 4 5 6 7 8 9 10 11 12 13 14 15 16 17 18 19 20 21 22 23 24 25 26 27 28 29 30 31

JAN FEB MAR APR MAY JUN JUL AUG SEP OCT NOV DEC

1 2 3 4 5 6 7 8 9 10 11 12 13 14 15 16 17 18 19 20 21 22 23 24 25 26 27 28 29 30 31

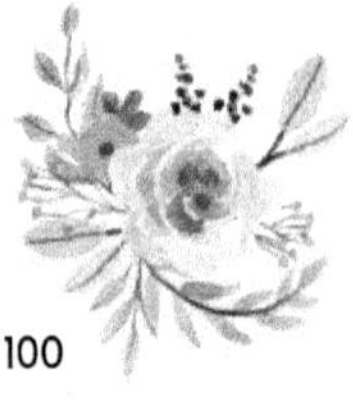

JAN FEB MAR APR MAY JUN JUL AUG SEP OCT NOV DEC

1 2 3 4 5 6 7 8 9 10 11 12 13 14 15 16 17 18 19 20 21 22 23 24 25 26 27 28 29 30 31

JAN FEB MAR APR MAY JUN JUL AUG SEP OCT NOV DEC

1 2 3 4 5 6 7 8 9 10 11 12 13 14 15 16 17 18 19 20 21 22 23 24 25 26 27 28 29 30 31

JAN FEB MAR APR MAY JUN JUL AUG SEP OCT NOV DEC

1 2 3 4 5 6 7 8 9 10 11 12 13 14 15 16 17 18 19 20 21 22 23 24 25 26 27 28 29 30 31

JAN FEB MAR APR MAY JUN JUL AUG SEP OCT NOV DEC

1 2 3 4 5 6 7 8 9 10 11 12 13 14 15 16 17 18 19 20 21 22 23 24 25 26 27 28 29 30 31

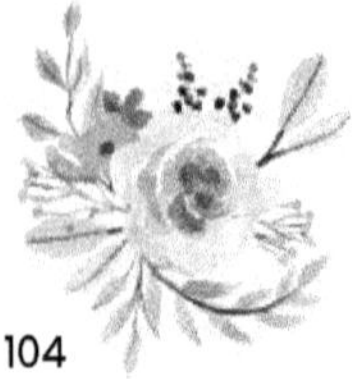

JAN FEB MAR APR MAY JUN JUL AUG SEP OCT NOV DEC

1 2 3 4 5 6 7 8 9 10 11 12 13 14 15 16 17 18 19 20 21 22 23 24 25 26 27 28 29 30 31

JAN FEB MAR APR MAY JUN JUL AUG SEP OCT NOV DEC

1 2 3 4 5 6 7 8 9 10 11 12 13 14 15 16 17 18 19 20 21 22 23 24 25 26 27 28 29 30 31

JAN FEB MAR APR MAY JUN JUL AUG SEP OCT NOV DEC

1 2 3 4 5 6 7 8 9 10 11 12 13 14 15 16 17 18 19 20 21 22 23 24 25 26 27 28 29 30 31

JAN FEB MAR APR MAY JUN JUL AUG SEP OCT NOV DEC

1 2 3 4 5 6 7 8 9 10 11 12 13 14 15 16 17 18 19 20 21 22 23 24 25 26 27 28 29 30 31

JAN FEB MAR APR MAY JUN JUL AUG SEP OCT NOV DEC

1 2 3 4 5 6 7 8 9 10 11 12 13 14 15 16 17 18 19 20 21 22 23 24 25 26 27 28 29 30 31

JAN FEB MAR APR MAY JUN JUL AUG SEP OCT NOV DEC

1 2 3 4 5 6 7 8 9 10 11 12 13 14 15 16 17 18 19 20 21 22 23 24 25 26 27 28 29 30 31

JAN FEB MAR APR MAY JUN JUL AUG SEP OCT NOV DEC

1 2 3 4 5 6 7 8 9 10 11 12 13 14 15 16 17 18 19 20 21 22 23 24 25 26 27 28 29 30 31

JAN FEB MAR APR MAY JUN JUL AUG SEP OCT NOV DEC

1 2 3 4 5 6 7 8 9 10 11 12 13 14 15 16 17 18 19 20 21 22 23 24 25 26 27 28 29 30 31

JAN FEB MAR APR MAY JUN JUL AUG SEP OCT NOV DEC

1 2 3 4 5 6 7 8 9 10 11 12 13 14 15 16 17 18 19 20 21 22 23 24 25 26 27 28 29 30 31

JAN FEB MAR APR MAY JUN JUL AUG SEP OCT NOV DEC

1 2 3 4 5 6 7 8 9 10 11 12 13 14 15 16 17 18 19 20 21 22 23 24 25 26 27 28 29 30 31

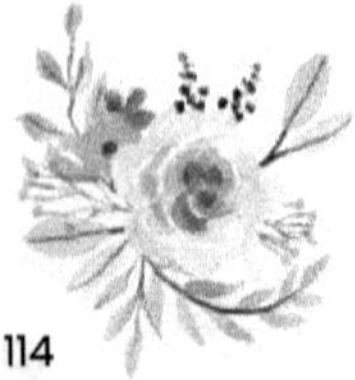

www.ingramcontent.com/pod-product-compliance
Lightning Source LLC
Chambersburg PA
CBHW072029290326
41934CB00012BA/3130
* 9 7 8 1 7 3 4 1 4 5 6 4 9 *